I Didn't Really Want to Be There

Why We Pretend, Remain Silent, and Stay So Long

Susan Gleeson, MD

Copyright © 2015 Susan Gleeson

All rights reserved.

ISBN: 1519181302
ISBN-13: 978-1519181305

DEDICATION

Dedicated to the memory of Ellen Faith Schouler (1949-2015), beloved elder and mentor.

Thank you for teaching me, Ellen, that we can always trust the suffering.

As far as you can, hold your confidence.

Do not allow confusion to squander

This call which is loosening

Your roots in false ground,

That you may come free

From all you have outgrown.

   John O'Donohue

   From the blessing "For the Interim Time"

   To Bless the Space between Us: A Book of Blessings

I Didn't Really Want to Be There:
Why We Pretend, Remain Silent, and Stay So Long

Table of Contents

		Page
Introduction		1
Chapter 1	Why we Pretend, Remain Silent, and Stay So Long	7
Chapter 2	Denial, Confusion, and Comfort Zones	13
Chapter 3	Fear	19
Chapter 4	Values	23
Chapter 5	Powerful Perspectives	29
Chapter 6	Finding the Courage: Breaking Free	35
Chapter 7	The Fallout	41
Chapter 8	Handling Freedom	47
Chapter 9	Mercy Is the Key	53
Chapter 10	Eldership Is the Reward	59
Appendix I	Personal Value Cards	65
Appendix II	System Value Cards	67
Booklist for the Journey		69
Bibliography		81
About the Author		83

ALSO BY SUE GLEESON

Healing Soul Misery: Finding the Pathway Home

Lulu.com

2011

If I Love You, Why Is It So Hard to Live With You?

Learning How to Create a Healthy Intimate Relationship

Lulu.com

2013

ACKNOWLEDGMENTS

I want to thank all of you who have helped me complete this third book in the *Healing Soul Misery* trilogy.

Joan Williams has been my editor for all three books, and I feel blessed to have her eye for detail and her ability to always "get it" working for me.

Thank you, Sheri for again helping me self publish a book. The best part is the fun we have together doing it!

Thank you, Dave Kerr, for painting such a beautiful and evocative cover illustration.

Thank you, friends, for reading, and for giving feedback on sections of the book in their formative stages.

SUSAN GLEESON

INTRODUCTION

This is the third book in a trilogy exploring the three facets of Soul Misery. These three facets are: *personal* Soul Misery, Soul Misery occurring within an *intimate relationship,* and now, Soul Misery occurring within a *system.* A system refers to a group of people numbering more than two, for instance: a nuclear family, an extended family, a social club, a religious community, or a group at work.

The primary characteristic of personal Soul Misery is *confusion.*

The primary characteristic of Soul Misery in intimate relationship is *loneliness.*

The primary characteristics of Soul Misery in a system are *pretense* and *weariness.*

Singer-songwriter Bruce Cockburn captures this worn-down feeling in his song, *Pacing the Cage.*

> Sunset is an angel weeping, holding out a bloody sword.
> No matter how I squint, I cannot make out what it's pointing toward.
> Sometimes you feel you've lived too long, days drip slowly on the page.
> You catch yourself pacing the cage.

I've proven who I am so many times, the magnetic strip's worn thin.
And each time I was someone else and everyone was taken in.
Powers chatter in high places, stir up eddies in the dust of rage.
Set me to pacing the cage...

Sometimes the best map will not guide you; you can't see what's round the bend.
Sometimes the road leads through dark places; sometimes the darkness is your friend.
Today these eyes scan bleached-out land for the coming of the outbound stage.
Pacing the cage....

(Cockburn, Bruce. 1995. "Pacing the Cage" *Rumours of Glory*. Waterdown: True North Records)

There are many metaphors for the experience of Soul Misery in a system. As Bruce Cockburn writes, it may feel as if we are a creature locked in a hopeless situation. Or, we may feel like a root-bound plant that has outgrown its pot. Just as this plant will begin to wilt, just as its leaves slowly lose their lustre--their shine and their gloss--so, too, can this happen to us. Or, perhaps we have reached a situation equivalent to "the frog in a kettle." An unfortunate frog can be placed in a pot, the heat turned on and then slowly increased. The frog gets used to the rising temperature oh-so gradually until he is boiled alive. He never saw it coming!

Other people in the system may well notice that we are not doing well, but it is not the *individual's* experience that primarily matters to a group. It is assumed that the individual will take responsibility for their own malaise, and then make the necessary changes. The system would prefer that an individual prioritise the needs of the system, and be a good system member by noticing and complying with the needs, values, and rules of that system.

So, when we recognize that we are suffering within a system, why do we pretend that we are doing well? Why do we usually remain silent about how we feel? Why do we stay so long?

I have learned that human beings are wired in one of two ways: they prioritise their own values, needs, and personal growth; or they prioritise the values, needs, and evolution of the system in which they operate. Of course, both are important, but--at times--our personal values and needs will conflict with the system's values and needs. We are forced to decide which is more important to us. If we choose to honour our personal needs, we can be sure we will come into conflict one way or another with the requirements of the system.

Sometimes our own personal values conflict when we consider how we should conduct ourselves in the world. For example, we may have personal values of Authenticity and Transparency that could lead us to declare that being a part of a particular system is no longer working for us, no longer meeting our needs. At the same time, we may have personal values of Kindness and Commitment that lead us to be acutely aware of others' feelings, so we continue our commitment to the group long after we have decided we would like to change our relationship to that group, or leave it completely. Just as feelings of Soul Misery in a system arise and intensify from remaining in an untenable system with no possibility of change, so can they arise when we experience an inner clash between personal values that are equally important to us. I believe that feelings of Soul Misery can escalate to a suicidal level when we cannot satisfactorily resolve a conflict between deeply held personal values.

One reason we remain operating within systems that are no longer satisfying for us, is that we are waiting for clarity. We may obsess over ways to "make it work," playing out scenarios that could possibly alter our situation. We ask ourselves, is there any way we can honour *all* of our values? Can the situation that feels so intolerable transform into something we can bear? We wait, and we wait, and we wait for something to change.

It can help to clearly understand the source of our deep inner conflict. We want to be kind, compassionate people of integrity *and* we don't want to hurt peoples' feelings. We want to accommodate others and their needs. We want situations to work for everyone. We want to belong. But we also have needs of our own and we want what is best for our own souls. We long to be who we are, to be seen for who we are, and to make decisions and take action that come from who we are.

Usually, it simply is not possible to honour all of these things; we must make a choice. Sometimes we choose to stay within a system that feels deeply unsatisfying for us and we end up sacrificing our very Self. Sometimes we choose to leave the system and we must suffer the social consequences reserved for those who dare to leave. Neither path is easy!

In this book, I plan to explore some of the reasons we stay in an unsatisfactory situation for so long--often year after year—while inside we are experiencing ever-deepening Soul Misery. The reasons are many; however, if we can understand something about the ones that apply to us, this insight may help us make the decision to remain where we are, or to leave the system in favour of something more personally sustaining. Or, new insight may move us to try to redesign our relationships with those within the system. Of course, this is only possible if those individuals are ready, willing, and able to collaborate with us in making the changes we must make if we are to relieve our Soul Misery.

I will discuss how we find the courage to make a change, and how we go about breaking free from our root-bound situation. We will come to see that Mother Nature's way is *always* growth. We will be given signs that the time for change has come. In many circumstances, though, it is desperation that propels us to initiate change.

As I stated above, if we decide to leave a system that does not serve us, there will be fallout. What, exactly, can we expect to happen? How do we find the strength and courage to deal with that fallout?

We find it by being aware of precisely what is happening to us. We find it by using certain tools to develop a helpful and powerful perspective about the *meaning* of what is happening to us.

Once we have come through the wringer of fallout, we take a deep breath, and then realize we are in a situation with few--if any--role models to turn to. We are going to need to look for guidance in handling our new-found and hard-won freedom. We must give ourselves the gift of time, patience, and kindness to allow ourselves to fully absorb our new circumstances and to harness new understanding.

In their book *Age-ing to Sage-ing*, Zalman Schacter-Shalomi and Ronald Miller explore, among many themes, the subject of wisdom. Answering the authors' query, where does wisdom come from, writer Joan Erikson says, "It comes from life experience well-digested" (71). We need time in solitude--time relatively free from external turmoil, to fully digest our recent, tumultuous life experience.

When we choose to extend kindness to ourselves, we are extending Mercy to ourselves. I believe the key to healing Soul Misery in a system is the quality of Mercy. Mercy involves, first of all, choosing to inhabit the beautiful perspective of Curiosity. Curiosity is inquiry without judgement. Having inquired into what has happened in a given situation without criticism, rulings or verdicts, a person of Mercy will choose to extend kind and forgiving treatment toward persons who *could be* treated harshly for breaking the rules of a system. How do we learn to be people who can extend kind and forgiving treatment to others? I believe we begin by extending empathy, compassion, and mercy to ourselves.

There is a personal reward for coming through the gruelling process of overcoming Soul Misery in a system. That reward is Eldership. An elder is characterised by wisdom, compassion, and stability. Elders attain these qualities by surviving an intense experience of suffering. These individuals learn not to resist pain, but rather to trust the suffering. By doing so, they grow deeper into personal dignity, self-respect, and grace.

As a result, an Elder is a person we can turn to for advice about the thorny issues of life; they have blazed the trail for us. Both the internal relief of *Whew, I've made it,* and the joy of being able to help others on their life journey, makes the attainment of eldership feel like a blessing and a reward, though the personal cost to achieve it may have been very high.

Come with me as we learn more about the situation I call Soul Misery within a system.

1 WHY WE PRETEND, REMAIN SILENT, AND STAY SO LONG

I was having dinner with a dear friend one evening. She shared that she had recently left a church that she had previously enjoyed attending. I asked her what happened. Why was she no longer feeling fulfilled, and how did she find the courage to leave her church community? Her response was candid.

> *I found myself growing more and more uncomfortable every time I went to church. I didn't agree with what the preacher was saying, and I didn't feel like I was learning anything new. The perspectives seemed to be black and white, instead of deep and enriching. And I noticed that I was becoming the worst version of myself at church! I felt myself becoming increasingly judgmental, critical, angry--and I felt disempowered.*
>
> *It seemed to me that preserving the status quo was more important than people, or God, so I made it my mission to change the status quo. Like a crusader, I tried to change the pastor. I tried to convince him that a new perspective would be better, and then I tried to rally people around my ideas. One morning it came to me... It wasn't my job to change the church, or the*

> *pastor's perspective. When I let go of the responsibility and my ego's need to change the system, I actually fell asleep! I slept through that entire sermon. And that was the day I decided to leave. Not because they were wrong, bad, or evil, but because that community simply didn't align with my real self. Or with my connection to God.*

So often we pretend to be happy in a certain system or group. It can astonish us to look back, count the years, and realize just how long we have been putting on an act. Why do we do this?

We may not even tell those who are near and dear to us that we are unhappy. We convince ourselves that we are okay--okay enough that we don't need to take action that would relieve us of our misery. We human beings have a strong ability to distract ourselves and simply carry on, that is for certain! So, let's challenge ourselves to make a list of as many possible reasons as we can think of for pretending, remaining silent, and staying so long in situations that have us feeling acutely miserable.

1) Confusion
We can't identify what is actually wrong. *I feel terrible, but I don't know why. I will wait until I know clearly what is wrong before I do anything.*

2) Bad Timing
We feel we must stay put until circumstances align and make it a more favourable time to make a change; the timing is just not right. *I need the money. I can't afford to leave. My kids are little. They aren't old enough to understand or deal with my changes. I don't yet have the skills I need to make a change and handle things on the other side. I will make a change, but not just yet.*

3) Things Will Work Out
We feel if we "hang in there," things could get better. *I'll just give it time. Maybe I don't need to go through the pain of trying to understand and make a change.*

4) Conflicting Personal Values
Making a change would be at odds with a deeply held value, such as commitment. *At the time I made my commitment, I was sure I could keep it. "A person's word is their bond." I couldn't live with myself if I didn't honour my value of commitment.*

5) Denial
Sometimes it is simply terrifying to acknowledge to ourselves just how unhappy we are because the ramifications are significant: we would have to make a big change, and that is scary! *I'm fine, everything's fine, really it is.* We believe our own lies!

6) Lack of Knowledge About Who We Are and What We Need
Sometimes we think there must be something wrong with us. No one else in the system seems to be unhappy. Everybody else seems fine. *Any reasonable person would be happy to be here. There must be something wrong with me. Am I crazy?*

7) Fear of Hurting Others
Sometimes we are aware that if we make a change, others in the system will suffer emotionally, and we don't want to be the cause of that. *Will my partner/other family member/business partner survive emotionally if I make a change?*

8) Fear of Disapproval and Rejection
Sometimes we fear emotional rejection and worry that a change could lead to long-term emotional rejection by others. *They will hate me forever. I couldn't stand that.*

9) Lack of Awareness About the Stages of Adult Growth and Development

Sometimes we aren't aware that human beings need to grow and develop, and the call to take the next step of personal growth involves discomfort--if not a degree of suffering. We judge ourselves harshly. *I'm a grown up, I should be able to put up with things as they are.*

10) Fear of Losing Privileges

Sometimes we are afraid of the practical losses that could/will occur if we leave our situation. We could be rejected--even shunned by the group, and lose all the privileges and perks of membership that we currently enjoy. We could lose a sense of belonging, and the safety and security of being part of a system. The thought of that is worse than the thought of remaining deeply unhappy. *I can't face all the losses that go with giving up belonging and going it alone.*

11) Lack of Awareness About Alternatives

Sometimes we don't know what we want instead. We have never had help to imagine and explore the alternatives. We don't know, for sure, that things would be better in another situation. *I know I am miserable here, but I don't know what I want. And how do I know that things would be better doing something else?*

12) Lack of Relationship Skills Required to Speak Our Needs

Sometimes we don't know how to go about confrontation--speaking our needs clearly and getting what we need. *They'll kill me if I talk about what I need and want.*

13) Comfort Zones: Familiarity With Our Role

Sometimes we are so familiar with the role we are in, such as "caregiver" or "rescuer," we don't know who we would be if we rejected this comfortably recognizable role. *If I were not a caregiver, who would I be?* And sometimes we aren't aware we are stuck in a role.

14) Being At Ease With Feeling Confused
Sometimes we simply allow ourselves to stay confused because if we let ourselves know how badly we actually feel, we would have to take action to change it. *I thought I knew how I felt, but I guess I don't really. Some days I think I can see what I want and how I feel, but some days I can't.*

15) Internal Conflict Between Two or More Important Personal Values
Sometimes aspects of our personal code of ethics (system of values) appear to collide one with the other. *I want to be authentic and transparent, and I want to be a person who keeps commitments, and I want to be kind to others. I can't see how I can achieve all of these things in my situation.*

16) Deadly Assumptions
We make assumptions. We assume there are no options for change, when, in fact a change in our perspective on a situation presents unforeseen alternatives and choices. *There is no hope for me. Nothing can improve. My only option is suicide to relieve my pain.*

17) Status Quo as a Familiar and Powerful Force
Sometimes we are so familiar with the situation we are in--miserable as it may be for us--it seems easier to just stay put. The status quo is a mighty influence! *I have stood it this long, I can keep going. There is no need really to go through the pain of making a change.*

18) Financial Fears
Sometimes we do not believe we will ever have the financial wherewithal to make the needed change. *I don't have the money to do it. After I leave the system, I will no longer have enough money to survive. I am really stuck here.*

19) Parental Concerns
We care a lot about what our family of origin, especially our parents, think about our life choices. *My parents would disown me if I made this change.*

20) Misery Loves Company: Four Crabs in a Bucket

If there is one crab in a bucket, it will find a way out. If there are four crabs in a bucket, none of them will get out. One of them will find a way to keep the one who wants to escape from getting away. *I don't have the courage to leave the others on this team/in this community/in this home. They won't let me. They keep trying to convince me to stay and every time they make their argument, I am persuaded to stay for another day/month/year.*

21) Guilt

We don't feel we have a right to want what we want and need what we need. *I should be able to overcome my own problems and go along with the others in the system. I am not trying hard enough. I should be able to set my own needs aside for the sake of the group. What's wrong with me that I can't stay here?*

In my 13 years as a life coach, I have sat with many people who are experiencing Soul Misery in a system. I have heard people list various combinations of the above reasons when they talk about why they pretended for so long that they were okay as they were-- why they remained silent about their suffering and remained in a particular system year after year.

Of course, it would take more than a single book to examine and discuss each reason in detail. But why is it that any one of them can grip us so powerfully that we keep saying *No* to our soul's need to make a change? We will discuss this painful truth in our next chapter, ***Denial, Confusion, and Comfort Zones***.

2 DENIAL, CONFUSION, AND COMFORT ZONES

Denial

I had an interesting conversation one day with a coaching client. I had come to know her as a strong, principled woman. It was clear, as well, that she was the true leader of her extended family. This day, she was coming to grips with having to take action regarding a harmful situation in her family at large. She was really battling with seeing and acknowledging what was clear to anyone who was not directly involved in the situation. I asked the client why she was struggling so hard to tell herself the truth.

> *If I say out loud to you, my life coach, what I know is true about my family, I will have to do something about it. Staying in denial is keeping me from the pain of telling myself the truth. I don't want to have to face my pain! I just want to carry on enjoying my career and my family.*
>
> *I hear the truth in my head, and then I just flick it aside and focus on something else. I feel so sad. I need your support to face this thing. I don't want to admit that my*

> *parents aren't perfect. I don't want to be disloyal or disrespectful. But the sadness I feel makes the truth stay in my head. No matter how hard I try, I can't flick it away so far that it doesn't come back. I am going to have to admit the truth soon. And deal with the truth. But I sure don't want to!*

This young woman knew that as soon as she acknowledged the truth, she would have to take action that might result in a rift among her relatives. She was miserable, and she was tired of pretending that everything was fine, but not yet miserable enough to get the help she needed to rock the boat of her extended family system. She was choosing to stay in denial about her situation.

It takes as much energy and courage to disturb a small system like this client's extended family as it does to cause waves in a large corporate system. This is because there are powerful group dynamics at play. The following five conditions hold true whether the system is a family unit, a church community, a volunteer organization, a workplace, or any gathering of two or more people.

1) If you break the core rules of a system, there is a strong chance you will be rejected by that system.

2) If you value your relationship with the entire system more than you value your individual relationships within the system, it will be harder to consider breaking the rules of the system.

3) If the rule breaker places great value on their relationship with a system member, then rejection by that member will hurt a great deal.

4) If the rule breaker places more worth on their own personal values than they place on the values of the system, rejection both by the system and by its members will hurt less.

5) It is important to fully recognize the rules of the system, both spoken and implied. Taking the time and effort to make these rules conscious is constructive, in that if you break the rules of the system and are then rejected by it, you will not take it as personally. You are simply breaking the rules of the system and are paying the inevitable price.

The coaching client who was struggling with the truth about her extended family was aware of these outcomes. And she knew that her family system strictly observed one rule in particular: *We put on a good face. We don't tell the truth about our problems to ourselves, or to others.* My client also knew that if she allowed herself to name the problem, and name it to the system, she would face rejection by her entire extended family. This is difficult to come to grips with; no wonder she was taking her time about it!

The love and regard of system members for one another is generally conditional on everyone following the rules. Why is that so? As is often the case, we can discover truths about human behaviour in art: in poetry, drama, and literature. Take, for example, Marcia Willett's novel *A Week in Winter*. The character, Daphne, is telling her friend, Maudie, that nobody likes it when someone comes along and changes the established order.

> *Are you only just learning that if someone steps aside from the herd he is likely to be torn to pieces? We're all so insecure, you see. If you behave differently from me, I either have to question my own beliefs and habits or prove that you are wrong. Misguided, stupid, ill-bred, it doesn't really matter how I label you so long as I can continue to feel complacent and safe. You have come amongst us and upset the apple cart (18).*

This passage reminds me of something a wise friend once said. I had asked him what he thinks people mean when they say, *I love you*. At the time, his reply seemed a little cynical to me, but in the context of considering rule-breakers and rejection, my friend's perspective may well apply. His definition went like this: When people say *I love you*, they mean *as long as you continue to make my life more pleasurable, you will continue to remain in my favour*. Ouch! Nonetheless, this frank characterization of romantic relationship does seem to fit with what we observe in human behaviour, at least some of the time.

We all hope to receive unconditional love--love that comes to us simply because we *are*. This longing comes from deep within us, from our souls. And we can feel deeply miserable when we are not seen, loved, and accepted for who we *are*, apart from anything we *do*. Of course, the unconditional love we long for can come only from our Creator, the one who made us, who made our beautiful souls with their unique design and calling.

I believe this longing is the source of much of our angst. Should we be more realistic and realize that human love *is* conditional, and will--in all likelihood--be withdrawn from us if we make choices and take actions that make other people's lives less pleasurable for them?

Our souls call us to make choices that will help us realize our original design and true purpose. It takes a lot of courage to strike out and follow the call of our soul, rather than to continue seeking human approval and love. Once we realize that the love of other humans is conditional, we may find the courage to be less dependent on it. We may find the courage to make the changes we are obliged to make if we are to be in alignment with our soul.

Writer, James Hollis is a great champion for valuing our individual soul's journey above the acceptance of the group. He writes in *Hauntings,* "Families are healthiest when they serve as launching pads for each person en route to his or her separate journey; they are most pathogenic when this project is subverted by its most narcissistically needy members or by the collective timidity of others to grow up, show up, and strike off on their own separate journey" (124).

When we come to the place in our own experience where we know we need to strike out on our own journey, this action may feel a little easier when we recognize that the love and approval of the people around us has always been, is--and will always be--conditional on our making *their* lives more pleasurable for *them.* We can choose to be realistic about this fact and learn to disconnect--at least somewhat--from needing others' approval for the sake of choosing to act in accordance with our soul's demands and desires.

Confusion

In addition to denial, another factor that can make it difficult for us to make changes in our lives is feeling confused about which actions to take. For me, the cousin, or precursor of denial, is confusion. Confusion really doesn't know what is wrong. Denial does, but chooses not to face things square on.

Where does confusion come from? It comes from fear. Fear that if we really allow ourselves to know what we want, we will have to act on that knowing. A friend and I came up with a word that we think describes the time when we allow ourselves to know what our soul genuinely desires. "Germiny" is when we decide to sow the seed of that knowing and let ourselves water that seed. It is a fragile, sweet, vulnerable time when we need to protect ourselves and reach out to dear ones who we know will support and love us. We have to give up what is known and comfortable to us for the sake of creating "the space inside" wherein the next stage of our journey will be revealed to us. It is imperative that we set an intention for ourselves: *I intend to allow myself to know what is next...realizing that when I know, I will need to act.* When we fully comprehend what is true for us, it certainly makes it easier for us to commit to action. Confusion--not knowing--is our true enemy because it can keep us in limbo for a long time.

Comfort Zones

A third factor that holds us back from making a needed change is our tendency toward habitual comfort zones. Comfort zones are actions or activities that support our denial by distracting us. We watch TV; we spend hours online; we drink heavily; we eat to excess; we even become obsessed with a positive action like exercise, all to keep us from the full knowledge of what is wrong in our lives.

Knowing there is something wrong, and feeling the acute pain of that, is what compels us to call for the help of a counsellor, a life coach, or a therapist. We must believe there are options and alternatives to what we are currently experiencing, even if we don't know what they are. Hope and belief in a better future propels us to learn how to make change happen in a way that preserves the humanity of each person involved. We *can* honour our own values and needs, and at the same time, respect the values and needs of others. This doesn't mean other people will necessarily approve of our choices. We will, after all, temporarily be making their lives less pleasurable, but it *is* possible to act in such a way that each person can retain their personal dignity and self-respect.

What keeps us from moving forward in this way? What blocks us from feeling hope and trust in a better future? Trust's opposite is fear. I believe fear is the most powerful reason for our pretending, remaining silent, and staying so long in our Soul Misery in a system. This is the factor I will discuss in the next chapter.

3 FEAR

When we contemplate making a big change in our lives, even if it is to relieve soul-crushing Soul Misery, we can feel tremendous fear. Fear of what others will think of us. Fear of losing their approval. Fear of outright rejection. We may fear the loss of position and status. We may fear losing money, or losing our job. We may fear *what comes next*, and feel anxious about not knowing what comes next in advance of making a change.

As one client said, "If I show them who I really am, will they reject me?" One teenager I was coaching even contemplated suicide. She asked me, in agony, "Is it really okay to be who I am?" Having coached many clients over many years, I am convinced that our desire for security and approval directs most of our choices in life. But in order to truly grow, we must be able to tolerate taking risks. While making the safe choice can help us feel better initially, this choice may eventually lead to us feel boxed in, if not imprisoned. If we are to fully develop our personal strengths we need: 1) options to choose from 2) an opportunity to try things out, and 3) the freedom to fail, which in turn, provides us with the chance to learn how to recover.

Institutions exist to maintain the status quo, and those in charge either know this and don't speak of it, or they don't know it. This leads individuals who function within the rules and mores of an institution to believe that life will reward them if they play by the rules. Sometimes, they firmly believe there is an unwritten guarantee that if they follow those rules, a reward is sure to follow. If this reward does not materialize, many such people believe they should receive compensation for their pain and suffering.

Rather than viewing pain and suffering as evidence that something has gone terribly wrong, I believe that experiencing pain and suffering actually can be an opportunity, or a gateway to transformation. There is no growth without suffering! Thus, to live in such a way as to never take risks can be deadening--perhaps a much worse fate than venturing into the unknown for the sake of personal growth and relief of your soul's agony.

If one does take the risk of leaving a group, an organization or institution, I think the most difficult repercussion is to be shunned. Shunning is severe emotional distancing and social rejection that a system can carry out when it perceives that someone within that group has done something to bring shame upon it. This practice can produce serious pain and psychological damage. The psychological damage will likely not be as severe if the one being shunned clearly understood the rules of the group, yet chose to break those rules. And yet, it is completely understandable to feel that we may be neither psychologically strong enough to bear shunning, nor able to build a new life with new connections that will provide sufficient, practical emotional support.

If we have belonged to a system that could conscience shunning, this is not a system whose actions we need to respect, or take personally. However, tragically, some people, with their mix of personal values, may conclude that the only way out of their Soul Misery in such a system is suicide. I do wonder if this is the reason for some of the unexplained suicides we all know about. This gives us serious cause to consider how each of us is behaving in our respective, various systems. Later, I will make a case for us to work toward extending compassion to those who change their relationship to--or leave--the groups to which we belong, even if we cannot understand such a seemingly contrary choice. I will make a case for us to become individuals characterised by the beautiful quality of Mercy.

Let's go on now to consider how values—both our own personal values and the values of the systems within which we operate – factor in to how we heal our Soul Misery within a system.

4 VALUES

As a life coach, I have come to see the importance of helping people become aware of their personal values. When we are conscious of the principles, ideas, and behaviours we consider important and worthy, we can see the reasons for much of what we do. Just as our personal values underpin our individual actions, so do various principles direct a group's collective behaviour. Simply put, systems have values, too. To discover why we may feel miserable in a particular institution or group, we must first become conscious of its values. Here are some examples:

- We always do what is best for the children. The needs of adults are secondary.
- Appearances are much more important than authenticity.
- We value diversity, equity, and inclusiveness.
- Our shared conception of God is the glue that keeps our group viable.

Problems arise when our personal values clash with system values. Picture, for instance, that you as an individual value Honesty, Transparency, and Authenticity, but that you are engaged with a system that values Appearances above all else. Or, imagine working within a system that values Uniformity, while you personally value Diversity. You can see that, depending on your personal values, you may do well in some systems and poorly in others.

Certain systems actually seem to give rise to Soul Misery, especially if the following conditions are present:

1) The majority of people in the system don't subscribe to system values of Diversity + Equity + Inclusiveness.

2) The system believes the needs of the system are more important that the needs of the individuals within it.

3) The values of Curiosity and Inquisitiveness are not valued by the system.

4) Homogeneity is a value of the system. There are rigid, strict rules for acceptable conduct in the system.

5) The individuals in the system possess a high need to be acceptable to the system itself.

Becoming aware of these values, and realizing how personal values and system values can diverge, helps us to see why we may pretend, remain silent, and stay a long time in some organizations, even though we may be feeling miserable there.

To identify your personal values, as well as those held by a particular system, it may be helpful to talk to a counsellor, life coach, or therapist. Speaking with such a person may reveal and clarify the issues that pertain specifically to you and your situation; it may also help you gain the insight you need to choose whether to remain in that system, or not.

As I wrote in the Introduction, some of the worst value conflicts are not between personal values and system values, but between co-existing personal values. For example, let's look at how personal values of Loyalty and Commitment could suddenly rub up against values of Honesty and Authenticity. Normally, holding these four personal values would pose no problem for an individual. But if we belong to a system that requires us to act in way that runs contrary to our convictions, conflict can arise. For the sake of our self-respect and dignity, we may need to be honest and authentic, but our positive feelings toward others in the system may compel us to prioritise the values of Loyalty and Commitment. *How do we resolve this?* We will discuss this dilemma and its resolution later in this book; for now, it is sufficient to emphasize the importance of being aware of, and familiar with, both our own values and the values of the systems in which we operate.

I have listed common Personal Values in Appendix I and common System Values in Appendix II. In the first and second books of this Soul Misery trilogy, I describe in detail how I go about helping people ascertain their personal values. I will describe it again here for any of you who are not familiar with that process.

I believe that a person's values--the principles and ideas that are intrinsically important and desirable in their life--are inborn, distinctive to that individual alone and part of their original design. I have worked with hundreds of clients and I have never seen any person with the same set of values as another; they are completely unique to that individual. To ascertain values, I use a set of Personal Value cards. On a table, I set out five different cards to function as column headings: *Must Have, High Want, Want, Indifferent,* and *Don't Want.* The client holds the remaining seventy-five cards. Each one has a value written on it. The card could say, for example, *Freedom to Choose,* or *Honesty,* or *Peace.*

I say to the client, "Think about a deep, rich, and satisfying life. In that life, where would each value belong? Must you have this value for your life to feel deep, rich, and satisfying? Would it be a *High Want?* Would it be a *Want?* Would you feel *Indifferent* about it? Would it be a *Don't Want?* Place the card in the column to which it belongs."

I sit and observe. In all cases, the client knows exactly where each value card belongs. When they have finished, I remove the cards they have placed under the headings *Want* and *Indifferent,* as they are not of high enough importance to discuss further. It is important for me to find out why the client has placed values in the *Must Have* and *High Want* categories. It is equally important to discuss the values placed in the *Don't Want* category, as it is not possible for someone to feel happy and fulfilled if too many *Don't Want* values need to be adhered to.

I then invite the client to define what each value means to them, because I know people will define each one in their own way. I also ask them to tell me why each value would be necessary for their life to feel deep, rich, and satisfying. In my experience, this is also easy for clients to verbalise. I think people know at a visceral level what they want in their lives. They know how they have been designed; they simply have never been asked the questions that could effectively draw out such vital, but deeply buried information. At the end of our discussion, I read back notes I have taken as the client was speaking. This gives the person an overall report of what is required to have a life that feels rich, deep, and satisfying *for them.*

I ask the client to comment on any insights they gained about themselves while doing the exercise. I also ask permission to comment on what I have noticed. For example, I may point out that I noticed how emphatically they placed a card such as *Freedom to Choose* under the *Must Have* column heading. This client has discovered that in order to live a full, rich, satisfying life, *Freedom to Choose* is essential. They may experience a moment of insight when they realize that, until now, they have made most of their life choices according to what others wanted of them. It can be upsetting to a client, however, if they realize they are at a point in their lives when they can't answer the question, *what* do I want to be *Free to Choose?* I reassure them that as we progress in the life-coaching process, this will become more and more apparent to them.

Not knowing clearly what we want can adversely affect our lives, because we can find ourselves making choices and decisions based on criteria other than consciously choosing what we want for happiness and fulfilment.

I DIDN'T REALLY WANT TO BE THERE

The American writer, Barbara Sher, published her book *Wishcraft* in 1979. Sher has been called the godmother of life coaching because she understood that to get what we want from life, we must first know *what* we want. Sher stated that to deny ourselves this self-knowledge is to do ourselves a great disservice.

> There are plenty of hard-working responsible men and women in our society who do know *how* to get things done but have never felt free to explore themselves and find out *what* they want to do. Contrary to what you may have been taught, there is nothing frivolous or superficial about what you want. It isn't a luxury that can wait until you've taken care of all the 'serious' business of life. It is a necessity. *What you want is what you need.* Your dearest wish comes straight from your core, loaded with vital information about who you are and who you can become. You've got to cherish it. You've got to respect it. Above all, you've got to *have* it (xx-xxiii).

If you haven't had the opportunity to ascertain your personal values with the assistance of a life coach, I encourage you to do the Personal Values exercise using the list of values in Appendix I. Knowing our own values is key to healing our Soul Misery in a system. Another key is learning how to view our circumstances from a perspective that affords us choice and strength. Let's proceed to consider the concept of the powerful perspective.

5 POWERFUL PERSPECTIVES

There are compelling reasons to stay within a system that does not feel satisfying and, moreover, is leading us to feel deep Soul Misery. It can be disheartening to realize just *how* many reasons there are to stay... and to recognize how many of them seem to be very *good* reasons. Yet, we feel dreadful and we know we have to do something to alleviate this feeling. What is it that can free us and give us the courage to make a change? I believe the catalyst is finding the vantage point, or the perspective, that is powerful and life-affirming *for us*.

So often we stay stuck because we view our circumstances from a weak perspective--one that does not align with our personal values; one that makes us feel weak and unable to set boundaries or stand up for ourselves; one that does not contain a single clue about how to move forward. Sometimes we may even enjoy our weak perspective! If we "buy into it," we don't have to take action. After all, we may tell ourselves, what is there for us to do, but endure? But in time, there comes a moment when we look around and crave a powerful perspective—the one that feels right and true to us; the one that we feel excited and deeply encouraged by; the one that offers empowerment and holds direction.

It is critical to realize that we humans make a lot of assumptions about the circumstances and the people in our lives. In his book *The Four Agreements*, Don Miguel Ruiz goes so far as to say, "don't make *any* assumptions."

> Find the courage to ask questions and to express what you really want. Communicate with others as clearly as you can to avoid misunderstandings, sadness, and drama. *With just this one agreement, you can completely transform your life.* (End-sheet)

Transform our life? How could this be? I believe we are so used to being inside our own head and our own habitual perspective that we think our way of viewing something is *the way it is*. The importance of realizing there are many ways to view the world cannot be emphasized enough. Becoming conscious of other potential ways to view a situation or a concept becomes our opportunity. We are free to choose another way of looking upon a situation that may have been causing us inner turmoil.

This came home to me recently during a coaching session. My client had been utterly miserable in her marriage for many years, yet chose to remain in the relationship. We had a "breakthrough moment" when I asked the client for her definition of marriage. She said, "Marriage is when God brings someone of His choice into your life, then gives you the ability to stay with that person for a lifetime."

I was flabbergasted. I informed her that others definitely have other viewpoints. As an example, I shared my definition of marriage. She looked instantly relieved. This client honestly did not know there was another way to define marriage; she had *made the assumption* that her definition was the correct and only one. Simply showing this client that she had long ago assumed that her perspective couldn't be changed, and then sharing other perspectives, was life-changing for her. It gave her the freedom to begin defining other possible viewpoints for herself.

I DIDN'T REALLY WANT TO BE THERE

It is amazing how much we take for granted as being *the way it is*. A respected friend of mine said, "People become partnered and married with varying levels of awareness about what they want, and varying abilities to assess the compatibility of their partner." As well, we choose partners based on our own definition of an ideal marriage, often without considering that our prospective partner might--from their perspective--have a very different assumption about what makes a healthy, long-term relationship.

To illustrate the degree that perspectives can vary, I collected definitions of marriage from many coaching clients, colleagues, and friends. I noticed that events and circumstances experienced in childhood, adolescence, and adulthood can profoundly affect how an individual comes to define marriage.

"Marriage is trust and teamwork." (a man whose parents each demonstrated these values)

"Marriage is sharing life's experiences together." (a young mother raising three young children)

"Marriage is a life-long commitment to another human being. Ending that commitment never crosses your mind once it is made… Besides, neither of us is willing to give up our dogs!" (a sweet, family-centered and service-oriented woman in her 60s)

"Marriage is a contract creating a business partnership designed to accomplish the tasks of buying a home, raising a family, and saving for retirement."(a woman whose parents were a financial planner and a bookkeeper)

"Marriage is the convergence of physical attraction, connection, a shared spiritual belief, and an ability to navigate the details of life together." (a woman whose parents were devout Catholics and devoted to each other)

"Marriage is a legal right. It is the right to publicly declare your love and your partnership, and have access to the civil and legal rights that come with it: to be deemed next of kin, to be the beneficiary of pensions and health care benefits, etc." (a gay man who fought for the right to marry his partner)

"Marriage is the relationship where my beloved beholds me with the fullest awareness of who I am—and loves me in full awareness of my vulnerability, frailties and weaknesses, as well as all my strengths." (a sensitive artist/musician)

"Marriage is a cage, a legal trap, with no 'right' way out except adultery or death." (a woman married at 17 and living within a strict religious denomination)

"Marriage is the ability to live together as a couple on a daily basis within the principles of love, empathy, and compassion--committing daily out of free choice and without confining inhuman laws. Because I am choosing freely without constraints and legalities, I feel authentic, liberated, and loved, but most of all true to myself and my lover." (the same woman at age 60, about the way she wants marriage to be for her now, the second time around)

"I imagine marriage to be a coming together of two beautiful souls in deep openness that allows those individuals to be truthful to each other and have an adventure with one another as they journey together in life." (a newly engaged, beautifully idealistic young woman)

"Marriage is where an able-bodied woman passes from the ownership of her father to the ownership of her husband. She ceases to belong to the family of her father and enters into the family of her husband. The products of her labour, including sexual relations and childbirth, belong to her husband." (a radical feminist who adamantly opposes the idea of traditional, patriarchal-style marriage, as she defines it)

"Marriage is a safe relationship where we support each other to grow and live our lives around some overlap of a shared dream." (an idealistic young man, whose parents ran a business together)

"Marriage is an innately human pair bonding that often results in producing and raising offspring, provides predictable, dependable companionship and resource sharing, and contributes to social stability by allowing expression of otherwise destabilizing sex drives." (a very intelligent and sensible, practical man)

"Marriage is the conscious commitment to the process and freedom of love evolution." (a yoga instructor whose parents are still in love)

"Marriage is the *action* of two individuals choosing to nurture each other's spiritual growth." (writer and psychiatrist Dr. Scott Peck's definition, said by a woman raised in an alcoholic family and deeply, positively affected by 12-step programs)

Isn't it amazing how much we can take for granted as being *the way it is*? We've seen how asking people to define just one kind of relationship, a marriage, can reveal all kinds of perspectives. Imagine applying an equal number of different perspectives to, for example, a definition of work, or what a family should be, or how a volunteer organization should operate. We can see, then, the large extent to which our upbringing, our personalities, our gender, our orientation, and our psychological wounds affect how we view the world. We can see, too, that our assumptions about a particular system and our relationship to it can hold us ransom and keep us from living a more whole and joyful life. Once we understand that we can alter, or even change our perspective, how do we find the courage to break out and alleviate our Soul Misery in a system?

This is what we will uncover together in our next chapter.

6 FINDING THE COURAGE: BREAKING FREE

We do not want to suffer. In our early 21st century western culture, most of us resist opening ourselves to emotional upheaval. In fact, some of us will go to great lengths to avoid it. We cling to the hope that, if we ignore a problem long enough, it will go away. *If I just stay with things as they are, I won't have to feel pain.* As if to reinforce this position, it seems as though everything conspires against change. The status quo is very strong. Systems do not like change. Individuals don't like it either. It takes courage to break out of situations that we know are unhealthy for us, especially when we realize that this action will involve suffering.

When we're on the cusp of making a change, we may feel like a root-bound plant. When a plant's roots are densely matted and have no room to expand, the plant begins to break down. Its leaves start to lose their lustre. It begins to flop in its pot. When all the nutrients are used up, the plant will die. It is a gradual, but inexorable, process.

Likewise, when we remain in a situation where no further growth is possible--where there are not sufficient nutrients for us to continue to grow and develop—we, too, become weakened. The process of our soul and spirit's dying is slow, but inevitable.

Those around us will notice our loss of lustre--our shine, our gloss, our excitement for life. But because those around us are busy with their own lives, they may say to themselves, *I don't need to mention anything* to them. *This is probably temporary. They'll sort themselves out. They're an adult, after all; if they need to make a change, they'll do it....* And so, our colleagues, friends, and family go on with their lives. They don't want to become involved. And they don't want to suffer, either!

Yet we know there is a time for everything in our lives. If we tap into the larger rhythms of life such as the cycles of the days and the seasons, and into processes like the metamorphosis of caterpillars into butterflies, we may be more receptive to knowing when the time for change appears in our own lives. This need for change often seems contrary to "common sense," and against "the rules," but it is a very real and powerful force. How do we sense when the time for change has arrived?

1) We realize that everything in life has a beginning, middle, and an end. We sense that one portion of our lives is over and a new one is on the horizon.

One Soul Misery sufferer, dealing with the need to make a change within her family system, described how she recognized that the time to act was nigh.

> *I had a sense, a dull sense of dis-ease for a long time. Years even. When things would go really well for a spell, I would heave a sigh of relief and in so doing, I would hope to squelch that gnawing voice inside. I definitely heard a voice. One day, as I stood behind the locked bathroom door with the water running so my tears couldn't be heard, I looked at myself in the mirror and I was no longer recognizable as the woman I'd always known. I looked different. I sounded different. This new girl asked the image in the mirror, 'What are you doing?' But it was that other internal voice that answered, 'It's okay, it's not yet time. Everything in its time. Just breathe.'*

> *Fast forward a year. At this point I was fairly broken and feeling immobilised. As I lay on the floor for the umpteenth time, I remember feeling like I was about to flip a switch. I suddenly understood how some people become bitter, angry versions of themselves. I heard myself say, 'Okay, I'll just keep going and in 25 years I'll ask myself what will make me happy. I'll just shut down, get through this, and figure out what I want later.' And then I heard the voice again. 'Oh no, you won't! Now is the time. Just breathe, because now is the time.'*

2) You realize your own inner guidance is more accurate than the external advice you are receiving.

For a while, you have gone along with advice from others, but now you know it just isn't right for you. You don't have inner peace. You can't have peace if you don't do what your inner voice--the voice of your very Self—is directing you to do. In his book, *Finding Meaning in the Second Half of Life*, James Hollis gives us psychiatrist, Carl Jung's definition of the Self: "[that] inherent, unique, directive, intelligence that lies so wholly beyond our ordinary ego consciousness" (4). Hollis considers the Self in service to the soul, which is the part of us that longs for "meaning, healing and wholeness" (4). When the Self and the soul's intent are in line, we get the courage to break free from a situation that no longer satisfies us. We want inner peace more than we want external acceptance, comfort, security, predictability, and approval—all things our ego wants for us. We become desperate for peace. For instance, one man came to realize that he could no longer hide the truth about his sexual orientation. Even though he knew there would severe fallout from his Roman Catholic family of origin, he had to tell family and friends that he was gay.

> *What prompted me to finally come out? It's quite simple. I got to a point where I felt certain that if I didn't come out, I would die. The fact was part of me already felt dead. Leading an inauthentic life, or a*

life focussed on not upsetting others, was killing me little-by-little. I was losing optimism, hope, and a desire for the future. Yet as desperate as I felt, I still felt this flicker of light in me. I knew I had a good life in so many ways, and if this burden could be lifted, I could continue on my path with ease.

I also felt a hardening within myself that I could not stand. I knew my family loved me and I loved them, but every day I stayed silent, I felt resentment toward them building while my love was decreasing. I resented all the times I prioritised their needs while letting them treat me as 'less than.' I was allowing it to happen and I felt more and more alone over time.

3) We become tired of being root-bound.

Just as a plant grows to a certain point where it needs to be transplanted into a larger pot, we realize that growth is an imperative--not only for the natural world around us--but for our individual souls. We grow weary of our listlessness. We can no longer choke back our feelings. We want to have clear eyes, a confident posture, and rich, warm conviction in our voices once again. We want to be who we actually are; we want to be in deep personal congruence. We need to honour our personal values, and be surrounded by people who see us-- who "get" us-- and support us in our quest to grow, and develop, and be all we were born to be. One man realized that as much as he enjoyed working with his parents and contributing to the family business, it was time to strike out on his own and do work that felt more personally fulfilling.

My dad immigrated to Canada and made it as a successful restaurateur. He dreamed that I would take over the restaurant and did everything in his power to make that happen. He primarily used the lure of money to convince me. As a recent university graduate, seeing all my friends graduate and get jobs, I agreed to join the family business full-time. His pitch that I could be my own boss and make lots of money was compelling. While he delivered on both promises, in the end, the restaurant business was his dream, not mine.

I knew there was something more calling to me, something that would use my natural gifts of easily connecting with people and inspiring them to be all they could be. I was also fascinated by psychology and matters of the heart and spirit. One day during the noon-hour rush at the restaurant, I got into a big argument with dad about how things should be done. That was the moment I realized it was time to step away from the business.

Walking away from a secure job was a very difficult decision for me as a male socialized by my parents and the 'North American dream' of having a steady job, owning a home, and achieving success in the traditional financial sense. I knew I needed to create my own version of success, and for me, part of that was to create a sense that I was using my natural skills and abilities to serve a cause greater than myself and my personal ambitions. I could no longer care as much about what my parents, or others, thought about my decisions. I didn't know exactly where I was going next, but it became just too painful to stay where I was.

Although it can be tempting to play the helpless victim and blame others for the situation we find ourselves in, thankfully, our souls will continue to call out to us again and again and again. We tend to remain within our comfort zone of the "same old, same old," but even a comfort zone can, in time, become a prison. Indeed, we begin to "pace the cage," as familiar and comfortable as that cage may be.

When we become aware, at last, that we are dying in our current situation, we build up the courage to make a change, which *will* involve suffering. We finally understand that we are losing our desire to live because we don't have the nutrients to sustain us where we are and must take action on our own behalf. Because in nature growth is normal, whenever we get into a situation where we are not growing, we are beginning to die. This is living contrary to both Nature and our own nature, and so, we do something about it. Note that we ignore the imperative to grow, whatever that will take, at our peril.

When the pain becomes too intense to bear, what happens most often is that one day, we simply jump off the cliff! It is said we must believe that either we will be given wings to fly, or that something down below will catch us. But most often, we just jump, not knowing for sure what will happen next. Most people experiencing Soul Misery in a system have been feeling inauthentic--their actions not congruent with who they truly are--for many years. We know it is time to transform ourselves and our situation, but who can really name the force that ultimately propels us over the edge of change? It would help, of course, if we knew there would be supportive people on the other side, but if we knew that in advance we would have made our change much earlier. It is the not knowing and the fear of people's reactions that hold us back. Thus, anyone who has had the courage to take the step to relieve their Soul Misery is to be respected and commended. At the same time, we need to remember that far from being better and stronger than the rest of us, the truth is they probably made the change they needed to make out of sheer desperation.

Having taken our leap of faith, what can we expect next? We will experience the consequences of our decision and this is what we will discuss in our next chapter.

7 THE FALLOUT

We did it! We made the changes we needed to make. We jumped over the edge. What happens now?

First of all, there is a feeling of exhilaration. The intense Soul Misery we were dealing with, and were so familiar with, is relieved immediately. This is confirmation that, indeed, the changes we have just made were utterly necessary for our soul's wellbeing. The sky looks bluer, the birds sing more sweetly, and the grass is greener as we walk with a song of joy in our heart.

It is important to remember these feelings of exhilaration, of relief and freedom, as we will need to refer to this memory in the days ahead. The stage of "happy liberation" may last only a day or two as the fallout of our decision begins to make itself apparent. *Fallout? What fallout?* Isn't the relief we feel enough to guarantee our long-term happiness?

The fallout comes from realizing that, although we have gained peace for our Self, we have lost approval from the system. And not only have we lost the approval of the system, we may actually be vilified by it. The system wants its members to prioritise the needs of the group, not one's individual needs. It wants its members to keep "the rules," not do what some of us need to do if we are to feel personally healthy and whole.

The individuals who remain in the group are put in a difficult position, especially those with whom we enjoyed a close collegial or familial relationship. How do they feel about us individually? What do they think and feel about our decision to leave the system? What do they feel about their own relationship to the system? Are they willing to risk the wrath of the community if they decide to continue a relationship with us? Each person with whom we enjoyed an individual relationship has to consider these questions. It's a lot of work--work that, in most cases, the individuals would rather not do. It would be so much easier if we would simply go back! And this is what most people will request strongly that we consider doing. If a large number of individuals demand this vociferously, the pressure to reverse our decision can feel intense.

But we know why we made the change we did. We are feeling so much better emotionally, mentally, spiritually, and physically. So despite the pressure, we don't "change back." Sadly, this means we may be rejected by many people, but as painful as this can be, it is wise not to take the rejection personally. As Ruiz says in *The Four Agreements,* we must continually remind ourselves not to take other people's responses too much to heart. Their response, Ruiz says, concerns them and how they view the world more than it relates to anyone else. They are responding from their own reality, beliefs, and values, which can differ widely from our own (Ruiz 1997).

What is the situation in which most people will tend to reject an individual who chooses to leave a system? If it is thought that a person has broken important rules of the system, and the majority of people within it agree with that view, then rejection will follow. Whether rejection takes the form of a subtle snub, a deafening silence, or blatant disregard, what follows is a period of grief. We have lost rights, privileges, status, and relationships--all in one fell swoop. Yes, we have regained our soul's stability and happiness, but we cannot diminish the importance of losing these other things and they must be grieved. They are every bit as real as the relief we feel.

As we grieve, we may wonder, why can't people be happy for me? I used to be so miserable; why can't friends and family members be pleased that I feel better now? The reason is, in most instances, they now feel worse! And because there is a good chance they did not know the depth of our misery, and perhaps are not able to feel Soul Misery as we feel it, they simply cannot make sense of our choice.

It is important to allow time to grieve what we have lost. Dr. John Schneider was a clinical psychologist and author of the book *Finding My Way, From Trauma to Transformation: The Journey through Loss and Grief*. He developed a helpful model for approaching bereavement of any kind. The Transformative Grief Model poses three fundamental questions that many people contemplate in times of loss. Schneider believed individuals must progress through three phases during which we grapple with, and answer, each of the following questions in sequence:

1) What has been lost?

2) What is left?

3) What is possible?

As we work through each question and make the discoveries necessary to move to the next, we will find greater peace and equanimity. We can heal in a healthy, transformative way. As well, Schneider suggested we may emerge from grief with an unexpected outcome, that once a loss occurs, an individual will inevitably evolve into something new-- something not seen before.

It may take three to five years for us and others in the system we have left to process and integrate the change we have made and find a new way to relate to us. Finding a powerful perspective from which to operate as an autonomous individual can help greatly during this waiting period. Once again, we are wise to adopt the second agreement in Ruiz's book: *Don't Take Things Personally*. We have no control over others people's perspectives on our situation. Nor can we control if they will *ever* come to accept our change. Often we are powerless to convey our viewpoint to people we love and value, and although time can lead to acceptance, sometimes it doesn't.

As people who chose to put our individual needs before the needs of the group, we can't afford to be naïve about the potential consequences of leaving the group. The fallout from taking that big step can be swift, intense, and even life-threatening if we aren't prepared for it. However, if we are aware of what form the fallout can take—if we can arm ourselves with a powerful perspective that helps us bear the time it can take for change to be processed and integrated, we can be more equipped to endure this challenging period with grace and compassion.

I believe the powerful perspective for this situation is humility. Our egos can insist that people *should* understand us and *should* support us when we need to make a change. After all, *we're good people and we have been there for them when they needed us. We have been loyal to them. Why aren't they willing to be loyal to us?*

A perspective of humility does not insist that people have to understand us, or support us. Humility requires, instead, that we know we are on our right path, that we are in right relationship with our Creator, and that we are in the best possible relationship with the important people in our lives. Then we don't need to throw our weight around, or insist on anything. When our actions originate in dignity and self-respect, we can treat others with courtesy and consideration. We can "let them be," and allow them their own viewpoints and the right to decide how they want to conduct their own lives—to include who they want to reject or accept.

I believe when we reach this position in our thinking, we are in the strongest possible place to wait patiently for the time of Fallout to come to an end. I love how the late writer, Phillip Keller, described humility in his book, *A Gardener Looks at the Fruit of the Spirit*: "Humility does not come from a position of feeble impotence, but rather from a tremendous inner strength and serenity. Only the strong, stable spirit can afford to be gentle" (166). We have to accept that some of the people we want to love, accept, and support us, never will. Thus, not requiring it right now--and maybe never--is the position that may bring us, and them, the most peace, self-respect, and dignity.

We *are* human, and we will struggle with how many people do not understand or support us when we make big changes. We may be surprised how few can do that. We do need some loyal individuals who are willing to stand by us, no matter what, and we may be surprised, too, by who *does* come and stand by our side, willing to steadily and quietly support us.

I believe these are people characterised by the beautiful quality of mercy. Soon we will discuss how important mercy is in the entire process of making the journey from Soul Misery in a system toward deep inner peace. But first, let's look at how we handle the stage that comes after the Fallout, the stage where we learn how to handle freedom.

8 HANDLING FREEDOM

We suffered greatly, we pondered our options long and hard, and we summoned the courage to make the changes needed to heal our feelings of Soul Misery within a system. We suffered again, this time with the intensity of the fallout. Now, circumstances and relationships have shifted and we feel a new equilibrium. We're experiencing less pain, and more dignity and self-respect. We are feeling more personal peace. We are also feeling the freedom to choose the course of our life from this point onward. But how do we handle our hard-won freedom? There are no rules to follow! Everything feels so new, we hardly know what to do with ourselves, especially as we have few to no role models. It is up to us to design our new world.

This liberty may feel overwhelming at first, however, managing our freedom can be an exciting and illuminating time for us. In his book *Eager to Love: The Alternative Way of Francis of Assisi*, Father Richard Rohr talks about the rich inner abundance that can follow a period of emptying. "The real power that changes people and the world is an inner authority that comes from people who have lost, let go, and are re-found on a new level. Twelve-step programs have come to the same conclusion in our time" (19-21). Rohr reminds us that Francis of Assisi and his friend Clare acted from this kind of inner authority. They chose to live their lives counter to the rules of the system of their day by giving up all need for power, prestige, and possessions. They lived among the poor. They let go of the fear of suffering the consequences of living contrary to conventional values. Clare, one of Saint Francis' first followers, came from a wealthy, prestigious family and abandoned her worldly birthright to found a monastic religious order, the Order of Poor Ladies.

The reward for both Francis and Clare was a settled sense of their personal worth. Their security came from trusting in their God alone. Francis and Clare endured a great deal of hardship, especially if we study their lives in light of Richard Rohr's definition of suffering as written in *The Franciscan Path of Descent*: "Suffering is whenever we are not in control" (cac@cacradicalgrace.ccsend.com, June 11, 2015). Francis and Clare each gave up any illusion of personal control. They tried to be instruments of God, and asked that they be "channels of God's peace." Rather than trying to avoid suffering, they embraced it. They lived with the poor and experienced the sufferings of the larger world. Francis and Clare didn't need to wait for liberation after death; they accepted their suffering here on earth, joined others in their suffering, and found inner joy and freedom. In giving up control of their lives--paradoxically, it may seem to us--they gained true freedom. Rohr says that, for him, to gain such freedom is to attain Heaven here on earth (cac@cacradicalgrace.ccsend.com, June 11,2015).

In her book, *Simply Surrender*, author, Caroline Myss, writes that the mystics Teresa of Avila, Julian of Norwich, Meister Eckhart, and Therese of Lisieux, all drew their strength from prayer, contemplation, and self-reflection. "They knew that a daily practice of time alone with God was required to review the day and reflect upon the well-being and harmony of their souls... The mystics knew the Divine through direct experience, not intellectual discourse" (vii-viii).

How do we learn more about drawing strength? How do we live with inner authority? How do we go about designing our own lives? Essentially, we look further within ourselves and toward our God to

I DIDN'T REALLY WANT TO BE THERE

learn how to live.

Learning about, or revisiting, our personal values is a good place to start. (See Personal Values, Appendix 1) Our values will inform us about how to conduct ourselves in the world. Prayer for direction is essential, too. Prayer involves sitting quietly, focussing on our God, being silent, and waiting--with sacred intention--for wisdom and guidance to arise.

Where we once looked to external authorities for guidance, now we learn to focus inwardly and find our answers there. As we practise doing this, we become more confident in choosing our own path, rather than blindly accepting that others know what is best for us.

In taking back our power to choose, we have also assumed full responsibility for our own lives. To help us live with accountability, it serves us well to pose some good questions for ourselves: *What makes me feel good and more alive? What fulfils me? With whom, where, and how? What gives me energy? What gives my life meaning and purpose?*

We ponder these questions with care, for the answers will guide and direct us. For a moment, let's use the metaphor of making a stew. It takes time to dice the vegetables, chop the meat, add the seasonings, and then let everything simmer until it tastes delicious. Similarly, as we enter this period of freedom to choose our direction, it takes time to ascertain which activities, which environments, and with which people to engage. There is no urgency to decide.

We have been accustomed to rushing through projects and focussing on achievement. We may have been people who were human "doings," now we are entering a time of "being." Yes, we will still dream, plan, and achieve, but we will do so with more intention and less hurry, ending up with results that are more likely to please and fulfill us.

Companions can help and bring comfort on this journey out of a system and into a new independence. They may be friends who have made similar changes. They may be people we meet at personal growth courses. God may bring them directly into our path, without our having to seek them out. Conversations with these companions can help us manage our freedom as we question them about how they learned to make new and more satisfying choices.

Ralph Waldo Emerson said, "We acquire the strength we have overcome." Going through the crucible of fallout burns off inessentials, and by enduring it, we become stronger people. It seems the more courage and strength it took to endure the crucible, the more strength we have access to.

In the midst of writing this chapter, I wrote to a mentor, asking her for feedback. Her letter of response was so encouraging. She concluded with these words: "I want you to know I support you absolutely personally, and I absolutely support you in your quest to write this third book of the Soul Misery trilogy." Her words affected me deeply because they are the antithesis of the rejection that can occur when one leaves a group. My mentor's encouragement made me wonder again, when people leave a system, why is the typical response rejection? I tossed and turned one night as I sought to understand.

The answer came to me as dawn broke. People reject what they don't currently have the capacity to understand, or what they choose not to *try to* understand. People also reject things that are too painful to contemplate. Finally, people can choose to reject a person because they simply don't know how to go about engaging in a process that leads to acceptance. I realized that it is not necessarily a primary goal for human beings to be inclusive, to accept diversity, and to seek to understand things that confuse them. It was difficult to accept this inconvenient truth, yet allowing people in a system the freedom not to accept our choice, is a key aspect of achieving a sense of personal freedom. It can be a battle to give up requiring that they understand, accept, and support our choices--as well as support and accept us as individuals. Yet setting people free to live their own lives and make their own choices-- just as we wish to be free to live our own lives and make our own choices--is the inner work that is necessary to set us all free. No matter who we are, we all want the same key things for our lives: *all* of us want to be loved; *all* of us want to be accepted; we *all* want to be understood; we *all* want to be supported; we *all* want to belong; and we *all* want to be respected.

How do we set ourselves, others, and systems free? How do we truly come to know we all desire the same core things in life? What is the perspective we need to arrive at this understanding? I believe that perspective is mercy. Let's examine this beautiful quality in our next chapter, "Mercy is the Key."

9 MERCY IS THE KEY

Mercy is the key to harmony in a system.

As we have seen, systems, by their very nature, can choose to treat an individual within it harshly should that individual decide not to follow some, or all of its rules. A system is essentially held together and bound by its rules--rules that often go unspoken, as is sometimes the case in extended families.

A system can have *empathy*, which is an ability to understand the feelings of an individual within the group. A system may show *compassion*, which is a sympathetic pity and concern for the sufferings or misfortunes of an individual within the group. However, it is a rare system that exercises *mercy,* which would show itself as kind and forgiving *treatment* of the individual within that group. In other words, a system can *feel* for someone who does not want to adopt all its rules, yet show them no mercy or flexibility. As one struggling sufferer told me, "You have to fit in, or fuck off." The insecurity of people within a given system, and the need for the comfort and safety that comes from compliance, can lead to harsh rejection of the one who wants to redesign their relationship with the system--or even leave the system, rather than leading to curiosity and a desire to understand and include them as individuals.

Co-authors, Danielle Laporte and Carrie McCarthy account for this situation in their book, *Style Statement*:

> Society sets us up to be right or wrong and rewards us accordingly. This is the very nature of culture and tribe. There is nothing especially restrictive about the times we are living in—in fact, in many ways today we are freer to be ourselves than we ever have been. But humans instinctively seek approval and comfort, so dualism—right vs. wrong, them vs. us, and more vs. less--is the lens through which we view both our outer and inner worlds (45).

Mercy is an action, not simply an attitude or perspective. Mercy is empathy plus compassion with wheels under it. Mercy operating within the heart of an individual who remains in a system will find a way to reach out, even if another individual chooses to leave that system.

When mercy is operating within a system, individuality is respected. Punishment for disobeying the rules of the system is not the default setting; rather, curiosity, empathy, and inclusiveness are the prized skills.

While I was considering the concept of Mercy, I had two encounters with the law within 24 hours. Late one evening, I was driving home, tired and anxious to get there. It was a dark, snowy night. Suddenly I saw the red cherry flashing in my rear-view mirror. Oh no! A police officer appeared at my window. "Ma'am, do you know what the speed limit is here?"

I humbly replied, "No, sir."

"Ma'am, do you know how fast you were driving?"

Again I had to reply, "No sir, I don't."

"You were going 80 kilometres in a 60-kilometre zone."

I DIDN'T REALLY WANT TO BE THERE

I apologised profusely. He asked me where I lived.

"About three minutes from here."

The officer said kindly, "Ma'am, I know you're tired and you're eager to get home, but please, pay more attention to the speed limit in future. Drive on now." I thanked him and pulled back onto the road, heaving a sigh of relief.

The next morning was sunny and bright. It was about 10 a.m. when I reached the country crossroad on my way to work. I was a little late and as I approached the four-way stop, I looked and saw no one for miles around. I slowed and at about five kilometres an hour rolled through the stop sign.

Out of nowhere, a police car raced up behind me and signalled me to pull over. When I lowered the window I looked into an angry face. "Ma'am! Do you know what you just did? You did not come to a full stop back there!"

"Yes, officer. I realize that and I am sorry."

"I have no choice at all but to fine you for failing to come to a full stop. That will be $110." And the officer strode off to write my ticket.

I realized that I had just witnessed contrasting examples of how people within a system, with agreed-upon rules and regulations, can choose to treat people. The first officer could have written me a ticket; it was certainly his right to do so. But he chose to extend mercy to me that dark night by giving me a warning. The second officer also was within his rights to issue me a ticket. He chose to do so, going by the letter of the law, because--to him--I had obviously broken the laws of the system. He saw no choice but to carry out his responsibility to punish me for doing so. The first police officer felt he had a choice to exercise discretion. The second officer did not. What determines our own tendency either to show mercy, or to follow the rules? I think chief among them is whether we are able to extend mercy to ourselves.

Christine Valters Paintner, a Benedictine monk and expressive art practitioner, introduces us to the concept of inner hospitality in her book *The Artist's Rule*:

> Each of us has an inner monastery, or cave of the heart. Inner hospitality is to open our inner selves to everything we fear and reject in ourselves—our painful and dark feelings, our shadow side, our resistance, the secret things we do and desire. If we embrace St. Benedict's rule for our deepest selves, inner hospitality proceeds from the root of who we are. We learn to extend a welcome to the stranger who dwells inside of us.
>
> Each of us contains a Self—the true heart of who we are and the calm, non-anxious core we all possess—that is able to witness our internal process. It is often called the inner witness. This part of ourselves ... can be fully present without anxiety and can offer radical hospitality to whomever or whatever knocks at our inner door (96).

Our inner witness is the part of us that regards ourselves not with fear or judgment, but "with compassion and curiosity—observing with love and tenderness" (97). To the extent that we can connect with--and operate from--our inner witness, that is the extent to which we can extend compassion, curiosity, love, and tenderness--without fear or judgment--to ourselves and to others.

It is easier to show mercy when we ourselves have been in need of, and been the recipient of, another person's kind and compassionate understanding. After such an experience, we understand that there is always more to a situation than what we see. There is always a background story and it is a story we may never know. An old French proverb says that to know all, is to forgive all.

Father Richard Rohr cites Jesus as a potent example of someone who knew the rules of the system within which he was operating, but chose to break the rules for a greater good. For instance, Jesus often healed people on the Sabbath, although the Jewish religion held that the Sabbath remain a day of rest. Rohr says Jesus respected the rules, but was willing to breach them for the sake of a larger and more essential value. This principled action, says Rohr in a daily devotional, is what Martin Luther King Jr. taught the American people and what Gandhi taught the British (cac@cacradicalgrace.ccsend.com), February 19, 2015).

As we have discussed, knowing and respecting the rules of a system, but then breaking them-- even for really good reasons--is never well received by that system. We know what befell Martin Luther King and Gandhi. They are revered and taught us principles of inestimable value, but at a huge price to themselves.

It is, therefore, a lot to ask of human beings to extend mercy to those who disobey system rules and values for the sake of honouring their own personal needs and values. Nonetheless, that is the path we are called to. It is important to remember that when someone makes the difficult choice to step out of their familiar group, they don't need everyone to understand in order to feel comforted and encouraged; just one or two people will do. Let us aspire to be one of those people!

Phillip Keller is a wildlife photographer and naturalist who explores the concepts of mercy and kindness in his book, *A Gardener Looks at the Fruits of the Spirit*:

> True kindness goes beyond the play-acting of simulated sighs and crocodile tears. It is getting involved with the personal sorrows and strains of other lives to the point where it may well cost me pain--real pain--and some serious inconvenience. The truly kind person is one who does not flinch at the cost of extending kindness. He forgets his own personal preferences to

proffer help and healing to another (126-127).

> ... As His people, we hold in our hands the happiness of others. The sense of self-worth, dignity, and personal esteem so essential to human well-being depends in large measure upon the kindness they receive from others. We have it in our grasp to enrich the lives of our contemporaries by caring for them in a personal, meaningful, Christ-like manner (135).

When we are characterised by mercy, we are on the path to becoming what our world really needs--elders. Our western culture currently idolises youthful ideals of strength and beauty, and we adults (as well as trying fervently to hang on to those assets) seem preoccupied largely with attaining status and wealth. But in studying adulthood and beyond in his book, *From Age-ing to Sage-ing*, Zalman Schachter-Shalomi looks to a definition of elder held by Psychiatrist and Clinical Professor of Psychiatry at the University of California, San Francisco, Dr. Allan Chinen. Chinen says an elder, rather than being preoccupied with appearance and position, "holds up an image of maturity that is based on self-knowledge, transcendence of the personal ego and the willingness to serve society as a mentor and teacher to the young" (140). Such wise adults can be found in our communities, ready and available to mentor, actively practicing tolerance and patience, mercy, and compassion. Let's look more deeply into the concept of Eldership in our final chapter.

10 ELDERSHIP IS THE REWARD

An elder is a person of wisdom, full of life, learning, and insight. Eldership is the reward for people who have fully engaged in the personal growth work of each developmental stage of life. We may believe that once we have made the transition from adolescence to adulthood, our growth and development have been completed, but this is not the case.

Bill Thomas, author of *Second Wind,* and Zalman Schachter-Shalomi, author of *From Age-ing to Sage-ing*, claim there is a further stage available to us: the transition from adulthood to elderhood. Thomas and Schachter-Shalomi believe that an inner imperative to begin this transition comes to us around age sixty. The transition involves undertaking a series of tasks, including such things as: life review, reconnecting with our 'unlived life,' forgiveness, and developing a proficiency in meditation. As well as completing tasks such as these, I believe there is a second, less-recognized pathway to eldership. Let's call it the crucible experience.

There are times when life places us inside a crucible--a high-pressure, high-temperature container that has the potential to accelerate the rate of our personal growth. If we submit to the crucible and trust the suffering that occurs within it, we can emerge as pure gold--having had that which is unbecoming burned away.

A crucible experience is one of initiation. We are moving forward into a new phase of life and, as when we are born, we cannot be put back into the womb. We are forever changed. We are living in a new reality and cannot step backwards into old ways of thinking and behaving. We can't have a foot in both worlds, the old and the new; we must move forward and inhabit our new world. As we discussed previously, Mother Nature's way is always growth!

Coming out of Soul Misery in a system is an initiation experience. We move away from the herd. We endure rejection. We suffer deprivation of love, of acceptance, and of support--all for the needs of our soul. We give up the desire to satisfy the needs of our own ego, or the needs of others' egos. If we experience significant rejection due to our decision, bearing the fallout essentially alone places us in a crucible of solitude where we must face ourselves without the pleasures, distractions, and comfort we have known in our former community.

The best-case scenario is that we emerge from Soul Misery in a system with a stronger sense of composure, identity, dignity, and equanimity. If this is the case, some of the people around us will see this and we will be recognized as elders. Our personal, hard-won, inner sense of self-respect, coupled with our ability to serve others by sharing our experience and wisdom, are the gifts we receive as a result of our crucible experience. We may well become a person bearing the characteristics of an elder: *a person of wisdom, full of life, learning and insight.* Attaining eldership can, indeed, be both the result of our hard-won freedom, and our reward.

Demonstrating the courage it takes to make a change + enduring the fallout of making an unpopular choice + doing so with grace, qualifies us to be an elder. Through the process of making change, elders develop a new array of qualities, values, and tools with which to conduct the rest of their lives. *What are those qualities?*

1) An elder is no longer a dualistic, black-or-white thinker. Elders know that seldom is there a clearly defined villain or victim. Instead, they keep their mind open to hearing the whole story, and even then, will seldom assign a villain or a victim role. An elder doesn't have the need to "be right," or to be sure they know what is right, or to force you to see things their way.

2) An elder does not make assumptions.

3) An elder does not take things personally.

4) An elder can see the meta-view, or the "big-picture" perspective of situations.

5) An elder does not separate people into "them" and "us." An elder knows that we all come from one source, as the rainbow colours that emanate from a prism all come from one source: white light.

6) An elder knows that the ultimate goal of one's life is to become whole, not to become perfect, and that the journey to wholeness continues until the day we die. There is always something new to learn that will assist our journey to wholeness, until we finish our life here on earth.

7) An elder knows that it is not so much what we do, as who we are that matters. An elder strives to be in deep personal congruence, showing the world a person who is presenting himself to actually be who he is. Elders have little need for managing the impression they make upon others.

8) Elders are people of trust: trust in God, trust in the process of their life, trust in the people who are placed in their lives to offer them service and companionship. Elders trust that their needs will be met in a beautiful and simple way.

9) An elder is characterised by a certain composure, cheerfulness, and dignity--with a willingness and ability to accept things as they are. An elder feels gratitude for the "little things," and for the sweet, everyday blessings of family, good food, and the degree of health they enjoy.

10) An elder no longer has a stony or stubborn heart. An elder has a tender, responsive, merciful, and compassionate heart.

These days, people are generally unfamiliar with the concept of elders. Aboriginal people still know and value their elders as repositories of wisdom, but I don't believe this is true of so-called "mainstream" culture. In "mainstream" society, there is no expectation that older people will become elders. Rather, older people are largely seen as having passed their best-before-date, and dismissed as having no value. They are often warehoused and ignored.

Such disregard is devastating for our children. One friend of mine believes that young people become addicted to alcohol and drugs largely because there are too few elders for young people to learn from. Young people feel there are few mature individuals modelling for them how they could choose to live their lives and few mature adults inspiring them to achieve their full potential. They search and search for worthy role models, sometimes among other cultures. Meanwhile, many older adults try to be seen as hip and young, rather than embracing what they have learned and considering what wisdom they may have to offer these vibrant, young souls.

Granted, as older individuals, we can choose to retire and do nothing. It is understandable to want to rest from our forty years of work as adults in the world. But people really do need elders. If none are available, our younger population can become angry or fearful. They may join militant groups, desperately trying to find *something* to devote their lives to and give it meaning. Tragically, it can seem as if there is no-one to go to for wise counsel and no-one to sit with them to discuss, and help them deal with, the thorny issues and questions of life.

But, in truth, there are individuals available for wise counsel. When something goes wrong in our lives and we respond well to it, taking adversity and suffering as an opportunity to grow, we are able to have more meaningful conversations with more people. When we survive a mess: a big change; a serious, life-threatening illness; a profound loss, or a time when we fail and then recover--we end up judging less, viewing circumstances more broadly and evolving into individuals who can show higher levels of mercy and compassion. Thus, more people feel safe talking with us at deeper levels. And when we have these meaningful conversations, whether with peers or people much younger than ourselves, we are now less certain we know what is best. We are more likely to allow people to come to their own conclusions about how to conduct their lives. As people in our elder years, we have a great deal to offer.

I love what Rabbi Zalman Schachter-Shalomi says about this stage of our lives: "A natural unfolding takes place in the psyche, which signals at a certain time when the accumulated wisdom of a lifetime reaches the state of overflow. Awakened to elderhood, we pour the distillate of our lives into other vessels, an act that not only seeds the future, but that crowns our lives with worth and nobility" (190).

Let us commit to becoming such willing vessels. Let us be willing to share with others what we have learned from coming through the crucible experience of Soul Misery in a system. Let us continue to live each day that we are given, considering it to be a precious gift. Let us be open to yet more personal growth and development. Let us be willing to be filled with joy and gratitude as we continue on the journey of life together.

Appendix I Personal Values

Ability to Influence	Endurance	Order
Achievement	Expertness	Passion
Advancement	Fairness	Peace
Adventure	Family	Philanthropy
Affection	Flexibility	Physical Challenge
Authenticity	Freedom	Personal Development
Beauty	Friendship	Play
Challenge	Generosity	Power
Change & Variety	Gentleness	Predictability
Comfort	Good Health	Recognition
Community	Happiness	Relaxation
Companionship	Helpfulness	Religious Belief
Competition	Honesty	Responsibility
Communication	Hopefulness	Risk
Conformity	Humour	Security
Connection	Independence	Self-respect
Contentment	Inner Harmony	Spirituality
Contribution	Integrity	Stability
Control	Involvement	Strength
Cooperation	Knowledge	Tradition
Courage	Leadership	Travel
Creativity	Love	Trust
Directness	Loyalty	Uniqueness
Economic Security	Mercy	Wealth
Elegance	Morality & Ethics	Wisdom

Appendix II System Values

Solitude	Diversity	Fairness
Professionalism	Autonomy	Feeling Understood
Ethics are Valued	Order	Mentorship
Eldership	Meaning	Equity
Connection	Silence	Rest
Acknowledgement	Friendship	Inclusiveness
Creativity	Cleanliness	Feeling Heard
Curiosity	Kindness	Sparkle
Deep Conversation	Tolerance	Teamwork
Clear Expectations	Accountability	Feeling Valued
Respect	Compelling Purpose	Learning
Vibrancy	Humour	Appreciation
Freedom to Choose	Competence	Change and Variety
Responsibility	Possibility	Challenge
Support	Space	Feeling Seen
Interaction	Competent Leadership	Excitement
Personal Growth		Acceptance
Freedom	Fun	Forward Momentum
Growth	Authenticity	Honesty
Interesting	Big Picture	Trust
Self-Expression	Laughter	Resourcefulness

BOOKLIST FOR THE JOURNEY

Beck, Martha. *Finding Your Own North Star*. New York: Three Rivers Press, 2001.

I found this book especially valuable early in my own process of relieving Soul Misery. As I began writing about how to heal Soul Misery in a system, I was led back to this book and received further guidance from passages such as this: *Transitions begin, deep down, the minute you set out to live a life that doesn't jive with your essential self. Over time, the dissonance, the sense of never being who you really are starts to bother you. A lot. In fact, it finally becomes intolerable. Even though everything may look fine to the people around you, your essential self is torn and dying. Either you end up having a nervous breakdown (which is really just your essential self refusing to continue along the wrong trajectory) or you simply decide that you have to acknowledge your real thoughts, preference, desires, and identity.* (247)

Borysenko, Joan. *Minding the Body, Mending the Mind*. Cambridge: Da Capo Press, 2007.

Dr. Borysenko has written many wonderful books, including *The Emotional Phases of a Woman's Life*. In *Minding the Body, Mending the Mind*, she discusses such topics as helplessness and denial, and she gives us strategies for how to overcome them. I gained insight about issues that can hold us in unhealthy situations too long because we feel powerless to change, or escape. Chapter 5, "Mind Traps: Outwitting the Dirty Tricks Department of the Mind," is particularly practical and useful.

Chodron, Pema. *The Places That Scare You: A Guide to Fearlessness in Difficult Times.* **Boston: Shambhala Publications, 2002.**

Buddhists say that attachment is the source of all our troubles. I didn't understand that concept at all until I was in a situation where I felt absolutely helpless to create an outcome that I really wanted. One day I realized that my attachment to that outcome, and my desire for a specific timing for that outcome, was holding me back. I decided to let go of my attachment to both things. Immediately, I felt in my body that a weight had lifted; I felt light and free. Within a few days the outcome I had been hoping for occurred, and the timing fell into place, too. WOW!

Godin, Seth. *The Dip: The Little Book That Teaches You When to Stick and When to Quit.* **London: Portfolio, 2007.**

Sometimes the reason we stay so long is because we don't know how to accurately assess whether it is best for us to stay, or to seek new ground. This book is fascinating because it describes in great detail how to decide whether a situation is optimal and sustainable for us--or not.

Hollis, James. *Finding Meaning in the Second Half of Life: How to Finally, Really Grow Up.* **New York: Gotham Books, 2005.**

James Hollis is a Jungian analyst, and in this book he begins to explain his concept of individuation. His ideas are thought-provoking, especially if you are in your late 40s or early 50s.

Hollis, James. *Hauntings.* **Asheville, North Carolina: Chiron Publications, 2013.**

Hollis is a champion for the concept that our main purpose on earth is to individuate--that is, to work toward becoming wholly who we are. I believe he sees this task as more important than being a good and obedient system member. Hollis invites us to ponder, *what does life ask of us, and how are we to answer that summons?*

Jeffers, Susan. *Feel The Fear and Do It Anyway.* New York: Ballantine Books, 2007.

When it is time for action, we need specific guidance regarding how to act and how to overcome our fears. This is a great "how-to" book for those times in our lives!

Keller, Phillip. *A Gardener Looks at the Fruits of the Spirit.* Milton Keynes: Word Publishing, 1986.

This beautiful book is one I return to year after year. The chapter on kindness moves me so deeply, and upon rereading it this year, I realized that kindness is the key to healing Soul Misery in a system. Keller tells us, "We hold in our hands the happiness of others. The sense of self-worth, dignity and personal esteem so essential to human well-being depends in large measure upon the kindness they receive from others." (134-135).

Kirvan, John. *Simply Surrender: St Francis of Assisi.* Notre Dame: Ave Maria Press, 1996.

Simply Surrender is one of a series of daily devotionals that feature writings of the great mystics of the Medieval and Renaissance eras. The mystics enjoyed joyful and intimate relationships with God, and they drew their strength from devotion to prayer, contemplation, and self-reflection. They are sweet, personal, beautiful devotional guides.

Levoy, Gregg. *Callings: Finding and Following an Authentic Life.* New York: Three Rivers Press, 1998.

How do we know the way? This book presents stories of people who felt called to change their lives and take alternative paths. It shares how people were pointed to "a way" that was authentic and "right" for their souls. It also lets us know that there is a price to pay for following those paths. This helps us count the cost and not be taken unawares when people resist, or downright reject us for going the way we must go. I found the Introduction especially powerful.

MacLeod, Hugh. *Ignore Everybody and 39 Other Keys to Creativity.* London: Portfolio, 2009.

Hugh Macleod is a brilliant writer. By means of hilarious cartoons and pithy writings, he galvanizes us with the courage to listen to our inner knowing and follow it, despite what others may say. As he says about soliciting advice, a*sking close friends never works quite as well as you hope. It's not that they deliberately want to be unhelpful. It's just that they don't know your world one millionth as well as you know your world, no matter how hard they try, no matter how hard you try to explain.* (1-2). Exactly!

McCarthy, Carrie and LaPorte, Danielle. *Style Statement: Live by Your Own Design.* New York: Little, Brown and Company, 2008.

Knowing our "Style Statement" can immunize us, or free us, from being stuck when we really do not want to be in a situation anymore. When *"following hard after who we are"* is a stronger desire than gaining other people's approval, we can set ourselves free. So often we can't free ourselves because we don't truly know who we are, or where we are going!

McLaren, Karla. *The Language of Emotions.* **Boulder: Sounds True Inc., 2010.**

This book explains what each of our feelings is trying to tell us. For instance, when we feel sad, Karla instructs us to ask ourselves, what needs to be released? What needs to be rejuvenated? As we allow ourselves to feel an emotion deeply, and ask ourselves the questions associated with that emotion, we are able to move through it and feel better, rather than getting stuck there.

Mindell, Arnold. *Working on Yourself Alone.* **Portland: Lao Tse Press, 2002.**

The concept of the spiritual warrior is found in this book. As Don Miguel Ruiz says in *The Four Agreements*, "You need a very strong will to adopt the Four Agreements." (23). In order to move from stuck to unstoppable, you need to feel desperate--plus you need to find the courage to change. Mindell says a warrior-like discipline is helpful in working on oneself and getting through a difficult spot. *Discipline is a subtle thing that you cannot develop by simply being interested. Discipline is an inner drive which pushes you.* (39) For sure, a certain deep grit and determination is what we need to make the changes we really need to make in our lives.

Mountain Dreamer, Oriah. *The Dance: Moving to the Rhythms of Your True Self.* **New York: HarperCollins Publishers, 2001.**

Oriah asks--and answers--the poignant query, *"What if the question is not, why am I so infrequently the person I really want to be, but why do I so infrequently want to be the person I really am?"*

Nepo, Mark. *The Book of Awakening.* **San Francisco: Conari Press, 2000.**

This is a book of daily readings that are as poignant as they are true. The reading for January 17th stopped me in my tracks because it so accurately pointed to the key conflict that produces Soul Misery in a system. *In effect, the cost of being who you are is that you can't possibly meet everyone's expectations, and so, there will, inevitably, be external conflict to dealt with--the friction of being visible. Still, the cost of not being who you are is that while you are busy pleasing everyone around you, a precious part of you is dying inside; in this case, there will be internal conflict to deal with--the friction of being invisible.* (20).

O'Donohue, John. *Eternal Echoes.* **New York: Harper Collins Books, 1999.**

I think I would have to say John O'Donohue is my favourite author. I can never read more than a few pages of his writing at a time because his words move me so much, and the content is so rich and meaningful. This book explores our need to belong. O'Donohue says the need for belonging is one of the most basic human desires and that it is a desire that "constantly draws us toward new possibilities of self-discovery, friendship, and creativity." His words can almost make me faint with the truth of them. For instance: "The true pilgrim is always at a new threshold."(124) Mmmmmmm!

O'Donohue, John. *To Bless the Space Between Us: A Book of Blessings.* **New York: Doubleday, 2008.**

This beautiful book is a compilation of poems and blessings to suit a variety of occasions. "For the Interim Time" is a blessing that, to me, seems perfectly suited to the transition out of Soul Misery in a system.

Paintner, Christine Valters. *The Artist's Rule.* **Notre Dame: Sorin Books, 2011.**

While putting the final touches on this book, a respected mentor recommended this book to me. It is set up as a 12-week program, teaching us the principles of what it is to be both a monk and an artist in this world. Working through the program gave me a beautiful way to ground myself as a monk and to see myself as an artist, writing and struggling to give birth to a new baby: this final book in the Soul Misery trilogy. Thank you, Julie, for recommending this book to me. What a gift!

Peck, Scott. *The Road Less Travelled.* **New York: Touchstone, 1978.**

Dr. Peck tells us that life is difficult. And once we see and truly accept this fact, life suddenly becomes much less difficult! He tells us that rather than acknowledging this fact, many people go to extraordinary lengths to avoid their problems and the suffering they cause. Dr. Peck quotes Carl Jung: "Neurosis is always a substitute for legitimate suffering. In order to solve our problems, we must be able to face those problems directly and experience the pain involved." In order to heal Soul Misery in a system, we must be willing to really *feel* our Soul Misery; this is the beginning of the pathway out of it. Though Dr. Peck wrote his book years ago, it remains so very relevant today.

Plotkin, Bill. *Soulcraft: Crossing into the Mysteries of Nature and Psyche.* **Novato: New World Library, 2003.**

As I began to read Bill Plotkin's book *Nature and the Human Soul*, I realized that in order to understand it, I needed to read this, his first book. *Soulcraft* is simpler to understand, and describes the difference between psychotherapy and soulcraft. It helped to grasp his idea that there are two realms of spirituality. The first realm, and the one we are more familiar with, turns us *"upward* toward the light and aids us in transcending our ego... So we can reclaim the inner quiet, peace, and wholeness of our true nature."(24). The second realm of spirituality "leads us not upward toward God but *downward* toward the dark center of our individual selves and into the fruitful mysteries of nature... We do not rise toward heaven, but fall toward the center of our longing." (24) *Soulcraft* is devoted to exploring this second spiritual realm.

Plotkin, Bill. *Nature and the Human Soul*. Novato: New World Library, 2008.

Plotkin gives us a complete, in-depth description of the human soul's developmental stages. We need to identify these so that we can place ourselves in the continuum and figure out our next task of personal development. When we are spinning our wheels, trying to figure out why we are stuck and unable to progress in our lives, this book can help us understand where and why we are stuck--and what we need to do to get unstuck and moving. There are no quick solutions offered, but then, we know there is no such thing!

Richo, David. *The Five Things We Cannot Change*. Boston: Shambhala Publications, 2005.

This book contains a wonderful chapter, "People Are Not Loving and Loyal All the Time." Richo explains how a mature adult responds to this truth. You can tell he is coming from 30 years of practicing as a psychotherapist; lots of living, learning, experience, and wisdom are found in his words.

Rilke, Rainer Maria. *Letters to a Young Poet*. New York: Norton and Company, 1934.

Rilke's famous quote about "loving the questions" is found in the fourth letter. It is a wonderful thing to read a famous quotation within the context in which it was written.

You are so young, so before all beginning, and I want to beg you, as much as I can, dear sir, to be patient toward all that is unsolved in your heart and to try to love the questions themselves like locked rooms and like books that are written in a very foreign language. Do not seek the answers which cannot be given you because you would not be able to live them. And the point is, to live everything. Live the questions now. Perhaps you will then gradually, without noticing it, live along some distant day into the answer. (27).

Rohr, Richard. *Dancing Standing Still: Healing the World from a Place of Prayer*. New York: Paulist Press, 2014.

This book speaks to how a mystic approaches the problem of what to do with people who don't want to fit into a system. *How do we regard them? How do we include them in our thinking? How do we pray for them and for us?* A beauty of a book!

Rohr, Richard. *Eager to Love: The Alternative Way of Francis of Assisi*. Cincinnati: Franciscan Media, 2014.

Father Rohr tells us here about the "alternative way" of St. Francis of Assisi. It is a beautiful call to following Jesus, without regard to power and privilege. It is a book that has the potential to make us feel set free!

Ruiz, Don Miguel. *The Four Agreements.* **San Rafael: Amber Allen Publishing, 1997.**

In order to make changes in our lives, we have to become fully aware of what is truth and what is not. Don Miguel Ruiz is the master of helping us know the difference. In dealing with Soul Misery within a system, it is absolutely imperative to understand the second agreement: *Don't take anything personally.* Once you truly understand why you are suffering, and don't take it personally, you are essentially free and on the way to healing/wholeness.

Schachter-Shalomi, Zalman and Miller, Ronald S. *From Age-ing to Sage-ing: A Revolutionary Approach to Growing Older.* **New York: Grand Central Publishing, 1995.**

This book is a beautiful call to an alternative and powerful way to imagine elderhood. It tells us that around age 60 we begin to feel the call to change the way we relate to the world. We want to move from "doing" to "being." Schachter-Shalomi and Miller suggest a series of powerful exercises to facilitate making this shift.

Schneider, John. *Finding My Way, From Trauma to Transformation: The Journey Through Grief and Loss.* **Traverse City, Michigan: Seasons Press, 2011.**

This book is about dealing with grief. The Transformative Grief Model is applicable to every kind of grief, including that which occurs when we are rejected from a system. The model is a powerful way to look at loss and re-imagine it.

Sher, Barbara. *Wishcraft*. New York: Ballantine Books, 1979.

Barbara Sher has been called the godmother of life coaching. I discovered her book after I had finished writing *Healing Soul Misery: Finding the Pathway Home*. I was amazed to find that as long ago as 1979, Sher clearly described the same process that--18 years later--Don Miguel Ruiz identified as "domestication" in his book, *The Four Agreements*.

Sher asserts that to get what we want, we must first know *what* we want. She explains that many of us are hard-working, responsible people who know *how* to get things done, but have never felt free to explore *what* we actually *want* to do. She tells us that what we want is not a luxury that can wait until we have taken care of all the "serious" business of life; it is a necessity. *"What we want is what we need."* (xx-xxiii).

Silverstein, Shel. *The Giving Tree*. Mexico: HarperCollins Publishers, 1964.

This is one controversial book! Touted by many as a shining example of how we should be willing to live our lives, others say it is a terrible book espousing a very unhealthy way to relate to others. I am in the second camp, most definitely. Read it for yourself and decide!

Thomas, Bill. *Second Wind: Navigating the Passage to a Slower, Deeper, and More Connected Life*. New York: Simon and Schuster, 2014.

I was at a conference and saw this book, newly published. Dr. Thomas is a geriatrician who began to observe that we can grow and develop beyond adulthood into elderhood. He saw the potential for a very rich and rewarding later phase of life. Dr. Thomas offers us a map for how to make the transition, which he calls "the second crucible." This is a very stimulating read.

Willett, Marcia. *A Week in Winter.* **Polmont: Headline Book Publishing, 2001.**

This novel documents, among other themes, the breakup of a marriage. In a moving section of dialogue, one of Willett's fictional characters clearly describes the very real state of fallout when you choose to go against the values of a group. (18).

BIBLIOGRAPHY

Cockburn, Bruce. *Pacing the Cage*. 1995. *Rumours of Glory*. Waterdown: True North Records. CD.

St. Francis of Assisi. Simply Surrender. John Kirvan. Ed. Notre Dame: Ave Maria Press, 1996. Print.

Hollis, James. *Finding Meaning in the Second Half of Life: How to Finally, Really Grow Up.* New York: Gotham Books, 2005. Print.

Hollis, James. *Hauntings*. Asheville, North Carolina: Chiron Publications, 2013. Print.

Keller, Phillip. *A Gardener Looks at the Fruits of the Spirit.* Milton Keynes: Word Publishing, 1986. Print.

McCarthy, Carrie and LaPorte, Danielle. *Style Statement: Live by Your Own Design.* New York: Little, Brown and Company, 2008. Print.

O'Donohue, John. *To Bless the Space Between Us: A Book of Blessings.* New York: Doubleday, 2008. Print.

Paintner, Christine Valters. *The Artist's Rule.* Notre Dame: Sorin Books, 2011. Print.

Rohr, Richard. *Eager to Love: The Alternative Way of Francis of Assisi.* Cincinnati: Franciscan Media, 2014. Print.

Rohr, Richard. *The Franciscan Path of Descent.* Daily Meditation. June 11, 2015. Center for Action and Contemplation: cac@cacradicalgrace.ccsend.com Internet.

Ruiz, Don Miguel. *The Four Agreements.* San Rafael: Amber Allen Publishing, 1997. Print.

Schachter-Shalomi, Zalman and Miller, Ronald S. *From Age-ing to Sage-ing: A Revolutionary Approach to Growing Older*. New York: Grand Central Publishing, 1995. Print.

Schneider, John. *Finding My Way, From Trauma to Transformation: The Journey through Grief and Loss*. Traverse City, Michigan: Seasons Press, 2011. Print.

Sher, Barbara. *Wishcraft*. New York: Ballantine Books, 1979. Print.

Thomas, Bill. *Second Wind: Navigating the Passage to a Slower, Deeper, and More Connected Life*. New York: Simon and Schuster, 2014. Print.

Willett, Marcia. *A Week in Winter*. Polmont: Headline Book Publishing, 2001. Print.

ABOUT THE AUTHOR

Susan Gleeson obtained her medical degree from Queen's University in Kingston, Ontario, in 1979. She completed her family medicine residency at Queen's two years later. Susan went on to complete a Master of Science in Community Health and Epidemiology, also at Queen's. She has now practised family medicine for over 30 years. Wanting to broaden her ability to heal, Susan became a certified life coach through the Coaches Training Institute; in 2006 she completed their Organization and Systems Coaching Program. Three years later, Susan completed the Coaches Training Institute Co-Active Leadership program. She also experienced the Bigger Game workshop led by Rick Tamlyn, and in 2010, became a Bigger Game facilitator.

Susan became interested in the expressive arts, and in particular, began to explore acrylic and watercolour painting at the Haliburton School of the Arts. She discovered the Expressive Arts program there--a program to enable professionals such as social workers, ministers, teachers, doctors, and nurses to integrate the expressive arts into their work. Susan received her Ontario College Graduate Certificate in the Expressive Arts in 2013. Along the way, she discovered Nia, a cardiovascular exercise program that incorporates music and expressive movement. Susan has become a certified Nia 5 Stages instructor and a Nia Blue Belt instructor.

Susan's other books are *Healing Soul Misery: Finding the Pathway Home*, which she self-published in 2011, and *If I Love You, Why Is It So Hard to Live With You? Learning How to Create a Healthy Intimate Relationship*, which she self-published in 2013.

Made in the USA
Charleston, SC
19 November 2015